ZEN AND THE ART
OF DISC GOLF

-\\\-\\\-\\\-\\\-\\\-\\\-\\\-\\\-\\\-\\\-\\\-\\\-\\\-\\\-

ZEN AND THE ART OF DISC GOLF

by Patrick McCormick

-\\\-\\\-\\\-\\\-\\\-\\\-\\\-\\\-\\\-\\\-\\\-\\\-\\\-\\\-

-|ZDG PRESS|-

ZEN AND THE ART OF DISC GOLF

[BY PATRICK MCCORMICK]

-\\\-

-\\\-

To:

My wife, who has supported me every time
I have said to her: "Hey, I have crazy idea..."

My mother and father, who assisted in teaching
me many of the principles outlined in this book,
many times without even knowing it.

All of the disc golfers I have met on the course who
became my teachers, with none of them knowing it.

TABLE OF CONTENTS

INTRODUCTION

"The big challenge is to become all that you have the possibility of becoming. You cannot believe what it does to the human spirit to maximize your human potential."
- Jim Rohn

Disc golf is one of the fastest growing sports in the world. Since its humble beginnings in the late 1960's to early 1970's, the sport has exploded across the United States and has continued to expand to more than 40 countries around the world. Today the sport has well over 7000 courses worldwide (as of 2018), and those numbers are still growing exponentially.

As a disc golfer who began playing over 21 years ago, I am continually amazed by the number of people out playing on our local course, the Bayville Disc Golf Course in Virginia Beach. Even early in the morning on weekdays, the course can be so packed with players that you have to wait in line to tee off on hole number one. Weekends and holidays? Forget it. Having to wait to tee off has not, however, extinguished my love for the sport. If anything, it has only increased my appreciation for it. Disc golf attracts so many people of varying age, ethnic background, and financial status.

What is it about disc golf that is creating such a "Buzzz" around the world? Is it the fact that most courses are free or only charge $2 to $3 to play all day? Maybe it's because the investment in the game is comparatively low since you can quickly begin playing with a single $10 disc (or even $5 if you buy one that is used). Is it because it is a sport that doesn't require you to join a team or a club (though disc golf clubs have sprouted up everywhere and are promoting the sport more than ever)? Maybe it is because it is a sport that can be compared to chess because it only takes a few minutes to learn how to play, but it can take decades to master.

I believe that it is the addictive nature of the sport that keeps amateurs and pros alike coming back day after day and year after year for more. Like I tell any new person I bring onto the course, "Once you hear those chains, it's all over!"

As I mentioned above, I began playing disc golf over 21 years ago, but I should say that I took about a 13-year hiatus (1998-2011) before picking up the plastic again. I was 14 years old the first time I played with my church youth group in the early 90's. Our youth minister, Jay Russ, brought us out to the Bayville Disc Golf Course, a course designed and constructed in 1977 by the father of disc golf himself - "Steady" Ed Headrick. We would venture there several times a year, during the summer seasons. Many times we came to the course in numbers approaching around 20 youths and a couple of adults. Other times, it was just Jay and me driving down to Virginia Beach to play. I remember the course being mostly empty in those days. You never had to wait to tee off. Most of the youths brought their own discs, Frisbees, and Aerobees (which inevitably were quickly lost in trees within the first couple of throws due to their ring shape).

If you would have told me in those days that I would still be playing this game in my 30's and writing a book about it, I don't know if I would have believed you. But here I am, fondly nostalgic over that part of my teenage years.

The first couple of times I went with Jay, I brought a basic, plastic, toy, Frisbee. I would do a run up with the disc and become utterly disappointed when it only flew 20-30 feet in front of us. Jay would select an actual disc golf disc from his bag and launch it down the fairway. I would marvel at the distance that his "professional discs" would get. I thought: "I just need one of those discs and I could launch it the same way!"

I remember the first two discs I ever bought with my weekly allowance, the Innova Viper, and the Innova Birdie. This was before I had any understanding of the flight ratings of disc golf discs. I was 14 years old, and I wanted to out-throw Jay (whose drives easily double the distance that mine covered) without learning the ins and outs of flight patterns or throwing technique. The Viper was a fairway driver with a vicious looking stamp of a snake on the top. If anything, a disc with a picture of a venomous animal alone was sure to help me outdrive Jay. False. Much like most people picking up plastic for the first time, I was disappointed and easily frustrated when the disc seemed to consistently pop up and fade hard left after leaving my hand. After several outings with Jay, the flight of my Viper never seemed to improve, but I refused to see the fact that it was not the disc I was throwing but how I was throwing it.

It was out of frustration, having to rely on a ride to the course, and getting caught up in the drama of my teenage years that caused me to quit playing disc golf.

Fast-forward 13 years to when I met my lovely wife, Chris, and we settled down in the Virginia Beach neighborhood of Chics Beach. My wife and I like to think we are active people. We love to workout, ride bikes, kayak, and find other fun adventures to go on. It was on one of our bike rides that I discovered just how close we lived to the Bayville Disc Golf Course. It had been years since I had set foot on the course, and apart from better tee-pads and signage, the course had not changed a bit (several years after the writing of this book, the course was redesigned and updated beautifully). Out of nostalgia, I asked Chris if she wanted to try to play a round one day. Always up for new things, she told me she would like to try it.

The first time we went out on the course together, we were armed with super light-weight Frisbees we bought at Petsmart. We played 18 holes and probably scored in the 90's, but it was at that moment that the spark of love for the game (or maybe nostalgia) returned in me. My old Viper and Birdie had been thrown out or sold in a yard sale years ago, so I went to the store and bought 2 brand new sets of discs, each containing a driver, a mid-range, and a putter. One set was for me, the other was for Chris or whoever might visit the house who would want to go out and throw a round. Little did I know at the time, after only a few rounds, a passion would return to me for this wonderful sport. But this time it was different.

You see, I never played many sports growing up. I was more of a music guy. Not a band geek, but a real punk rocker. I spent most of my teenage years and up until my early 20's with spiky, colored hair, sometimes waxed or glued into the shape of a mohawk. I was pierced and tattooed, I played in punk, hardcore, and industrial bands, and I spent most of my time writing music or sitting behind the control desk at a local recording studio. To be honest, I was generally afraid of sunlight. I went to college and earned a degree in business management because at the time I desired to open up my own recording studio and record label.

During college, when I wasn't in class or working on new material for my various music projects, I wasn't out playing disc golf, I was inside reading. Though I may have looked a little extreme or seemed like an outcast to the fraternity crowd, I had a healthy thirst for knowledge beyond that of my business coursework. That was when I discovered three books that changed my life: *Think and Grow Rich* by Napoleon Hill, *The Power of Positive Thinking* by Norman Vincent Peale, and *As A Man Thinketh* by James Allen. Those titles planted a seed in me which became one of my core beliefs:

Everything we experience outwardly begins inwardly.

Those books also made it plain to me that if we want to become enlightened and prosperous people in this life, it is beneficial to develop ways to practice watching our thoughts, controlling them before they control us, putting negative thoughts to pasture, and putting positive thoughts into action.

Once my mind became open to these ideas, I searched my Bible to be sure that they were backed up in the ultimate book of wisdom. Much to my surprise, I found evidence of these philosophies spread through both Testaments. This new (to me) philosophy now seemed to be solidified in my mind and spirit.

Sometimes we find everything we are looking for when we stop looking. I discovered my mindful (thought monitoring) practice on the disc golf course when I wasn't even looking for it.

Many times in conversations, I began making comparisons and using disc golf metaphors to try and explain my worldview and philosophy of life to others. Of course, it was usually met with the blank faces of non-disc golfers staring back at me as if I had lost my mind. They would miss the point entirely and get stuck on the fact I was talking about this "Frolf" thing again.

Then it hit me. I should share these insights with people out there who are more likely to actually get it – the hoards of people I see on the disc golf course every morning. This is how I give back to disc golf and the disc golf community for everything it has given to me.

I sincerely hope you enjoy reading this book as much as I have enjoyed writing it. It has been 3 years in the making, and I have forgone many rounds to put it together. That being said, now that it is completed, I'm off to the course!

All of the best for your life and for your game!
Patrick McCormick

IS / IS NOT

Before we get started, I would like to talk about what this book is and what this book is not. Let's start with what it is not.

WHAT THIS BOOK IS NOT –

This book is not an instruction manual on how to play disc golf. It is not a rulebook. You can find many tutorials on the internet on how to properly throw a disc golf disc. And you can visit the PDGA website to download a rule book. Believe me, there is no way that one book could teach you how to physically play disc golf. This makes me think of a person trying to learn some form of martial art from a book, never training with a sensei or teacher; it's just laughable. The best way to learn how to play disc golf is to hit the course, find some experienced players, learn everything you can from them, and practice - practice - practice.

Similarly, this book is not really related to the Eastern philosophy of Zen Buddhism. Though I have studied many world religions extensively, I am a Christian (as you may have concluded from my Introduction), and I have carefully researched the values in this book not only to be sure that they have some theological basis, but would work for anyone who practices them, and thus be of some benefit to the masses (at least mentally and physically).

So you might be asking: "If this book is not about how to play disc golf or how to practice Zen, what is it about and why did you title it *Zen And The Art Of Disc Golf?*"

WHAT THIS BOOK IS -

To be quite honest, the title was influenced by Robert M Pirsig's book, *Zen and the Art of Motorcycle Maintenance*. In the book, Pirsig uses a motorcycle trip and the maintenance of his vehicle as a mindful lens into life. Like Pirsig, my goal is to examine life using disc golf as a lens.

I believe that there are three aspects to living a balanced life. These aspects are the physical, the mental, and the spiritual. I have found that disc golf is such a unique blend of these three aspects, that if practiced properly on the course, your game will dramatically improve. I have also discovered that practicing these three elements on the course will have an overflow into practicing them in your life.

IN THIS WAY - DISC GOLF CHANGED *MY* LIFE.

As I mentioned in my Introduction, I began playing disc golf as a young teenager but took about 13 years off from the game. When I returned, the course taught me more about who I was (and how my thinking affected me) than any other activity that I have ever been involved with. Disc golf can become a mirror of yourself once you learn to step back and see that you are the game and the game is you.

The physical part of disc golf is obvious. It is the mechanics of the various throws and the navigation of obstacles on the course. As I mentioned above, the mechanics of disc golf cannot be learned from a book but are learned in practice. This book is about the mental and spiritual aspects of the game and how those aspects can transition into your life to promote balance and success.

Playing disc golf can help give us a window to ourselves, how we see the world, how our thoughts and attitudes affect the decisions we make, which in turn determines whether or not we will live successful lives.

This book is about being a balanced player with a positive attitude and in turn becoming a balanced individual that is happy in life and successful in their goals.

MOST IMPORTANTLY, JUST THROW.

GETTING THE MOST
OUT OF THIS BOOK

"If you can see yourself doing something, you can do it. If you can't see yourself doing it, usually you can't achieve it."
- **David Goggins**

If you are an avid reader, you may find yourselves feeling like you should read this book cover to cover in one or more sittings. My suggestion for getting the most out of this book would be to read only one chapter at a time, then go outside and play a round or two before coming back to learn more. This will give you time to have the information from each chapter sink in.

After each chapter hit the course, and "meditate" on what you have read. Ask yourself if your mindset on the course is a reflection of your mindset off the course. Try finding ways to improve your round, and ask yourself if those improvements have a practical application in your life.

Reading about throwing is no substitute for actually throwing. We are disc golfers because we love getting outside and looking for that perfect disc flight. Have fun. Learn something about the game and hopefully something about yourself.

THE THREE SIDES

"Prepare yourself off the field by exercising, eating right, and getting enough sleep. When your heart isn't pounding, back isn't aching, and dogs aren't barking, your body can focus on the task at hand."
- Liz Carr

The beauty of disc golf is in the simplistic nature of the game. If you understand the basic rules of golf, getting from point A to point B in the least amount of strokes possible, then you understand disc golf. The ball is replaced with a disc or Frisbee, and you try to take the least amount of strokes between the tee box and the basket. It's one of those games that takes less than an hour to learn but a lifetime to master; it is because of this you see all age groups from children to seniors enjoying the game.

In the last decade, the game has grown to encompass people of all ages, nationalities, and economic backgrounds. It has come from being a recreational activity to an actual, athletic sport, gaining attention on ESPN, and showcasing pro players who can whip a distance driver upwards of 1,109 feet (David Wiggins Jr. for the world record in 2016).

At first glance, the game appears easy or even juvenile. I think this is why many athletes and sportsman from other athletic backgrounds chuckle at the idea of grown adults throwing Frisbees in the woods. The other reason is the stigma that Frisbees have with the hippy movement of the 1960's. But those who give the game a try, see that it is not juvenile at all but that it takes skill, focus, and finesse to get that plastic in the basket.

Most first time players believe that since they have thrown a Frisbee before, they can throw a disc golf disc just as well. They have read the ratings on the various drivers, and they think that since the discs have distance and speed ratings, all you have to do is toss it like you would any "throw and catch" disc, and the disc will do the rest of the work for you. They do a run up on the tee and release the disc, sweeping their arm out wide and become discouraged entirely when the drive pops up high into the air and fades hard to the left. Without a mentor or seasoned player coaching them, they believe that there is only one way to throw a disc, and they do not see that their technique is their a problem but blame their disc for its poor lie.

This experience leads many new players to either merely quitting on themselves right there or going out on a quest for that perfect disc that will fly better for them. This new player may end up with a bag stuffed full of discs that they are fundamentally unable to throw because they never learned the proper throwing technique. I know this is the case because this was me. This was how I started, and I see it time and time again with other new players. There is a small, though costly, benefit to this pattern. Once a player learns that it is not the disc at all but the technique – you have now accumulated an arsenal of discs at your disposal. The setback is all of the money you spent trying to figure that out. Eventually, most of us find a couple "go to" discs and begin to lighten our load.

Most people's first round of disc golf is awkward. There are no two ways about it. The disc doesn't seem to fly correctly, they hit trees, lose discs, and can't even make short putts. This can drive some people to become extremely frustrated and throw their new plastic in the trash, but this difficulty drives others to practice and craft their addiction. They want to get past that awkward phase and throw 300-foot drives and make 25-foot putts. This was the class of new players I fell into.

Learning to play disc golf is like learning to do any other new activity in your life. If you ever had to learn to drive a car with a manual transmission, you remember the first few times you tried. You stalled out, the vehicle made loud grinding noises, and you rolled backward down hills until you learned to get the clutch into its sweet spot and pop the car into first.

Going back even further, when you were a child, you were required to learn many new things, and all of them were awkward at first. When you learned to ride a bike, it wobbled, and you fell, but if you were one of those kids who kept trying, you learned that once you got going, things got more comfortable. Children have an understanding that things sometimes take time to learn, and that is lost in adulthood. Adults want to be able to do things right on their first try time, without fail, and if they think they can't, they never even try. Most of the time, they quit way too early.

But what if you never learned to tie your shoes, ride a bike, or drive a car? You would have never gotten anywhere. As an adult, you need to come to an understanding that the rules have not changed; getting good at something takes time. It takes practice and hard work. And the more you work on something, the better the rewards. If success were always instant and easy, everyone would be successful, and there would be no pride in achievement.

IF SUCCESS WAS ALWAYS INSTANT AND EASY, EVERYONE WOULD BE SUCCESSFUL, AND THERE WOULD BE NO PRIDE IN ACHIEVEMENT.

Disc golf can teach you so much about life because it is a perfectly balanced game between the 3 elements of everyone's existence: the physical, the mental, and the spiritual.

To be proficient at playing disc golf, you must be in tune with all of these elements equally. I am sure many other sports and games involve these aspects, but to me, disc golf is different: You can play or practice on your own, anywhere, year round.

The physical part of the game is evident. It involves using your body mechanics to throw discs utilizing various grips and throwing techniques that you could never learn from the pages of a book. The mental part of the game is just as challenging because it is a thinking and focus game. And the spiritual part of the game is that with an open mind it becomes a walking meditation on who you are on and off the course. It gives you a practice for monitoring your thoughts. How you act and play disc golf is a direct extension of who you are in relationships, business, and life.

The more I have practiced disc golf, the more I have found that this active thought monitoring process and quieting the mind was essential to becoming a better player. I also began noticing the parallels between disc golf and life. And as I saw how some of my attitudes on the course were not helping my game, neither were they helping me in my life.

Disc golf has helped me fine tune my physical, mental, and spiritual self by acting as a window where I can objectively view how I behave and think, and how these behaviors and thought patterns either help or hurt me in my everyday life.

THE MEDITATIVE NATURE
OF DISC GOLF

"We struggle with the complexities and ignore the simplicities."
- **Norman Vincent Peale**

Doing something for someone else can be one of life's greatest joys. We have all been told for ages that "It is more blessed to give than it is to receive," and the older I get, the more I find this principle to be entirely accurate. People who strive to give of themselves are statistically happier and live longer lives. But just as with everything in life, there must be a balance. Those who give nothing are regarded as lazy and selfish and those who continually give of themselves, to their own detriment, very often become unhappy martyrs. Again, there must be a balance. Giving to others comes with huge rewards, but a dry glass can't quench another's thirst. This is why we must make taking care of ourselves in mind, in body, and in spirit, a huge priority.

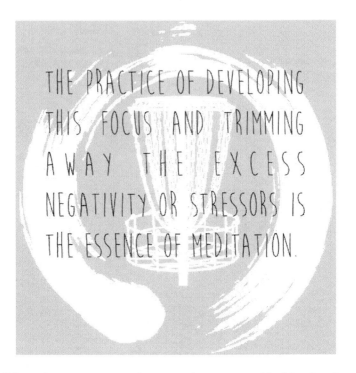

THE PRACTICE OF DEVELOPING THIS FOCUS AND TRIMMING AWAY THE EXCESS NEGATIVITY OR STRESSORS IS THE ESSENCE OF MEDITATION.

I have been out many times on the course with friends who say their spouse is mad at them for spending "too much time" playing disc golf. These are guys who are family men, who I know spend time with their kids and wives, take care of chores, and earn income for their households, but they are made to actually feel guilty for spending time, any time, to improve their games as well as their mental and physical health. These are guys who have their priorities straight but crave the exercise and the clanging of chains.

It is vital for us to understand that once we have our priorities straight, we all need time to ourselves to relax and reflect on how we are doing both internally and externally. We all need time to decompress so that we can give others the best possible versions of ourselves. If you are going to give of yourself, make sure the you that you are offering is a quality product.

Think of it this way: a teacher must spend time learning. A fitness coach must spend time perfecting their fitness. A preacher must spend time in prayer and study. A philanthropist must earn the money that they give away. Mastery comes first, then serving.

An apple tree doesn't merely produce apple after apple without taking in water, rays from the sun, and nutrients from the soil. You cannot bear healthy fruit for yourself or others if you never take the time to focus on the things that help you to grow either. Becoming a martyr is selfish. To sacrifice your own happiness and give world around you lousy fruit because you have not taken time for your own personal growth. It is much better to provide the world with good sweet fruit than fruit that has gone bad through neglect.

When we eat, we nourish the body. When we study, we nourish the mind. When we meditate, pray, or try to become the best possible version of ourselves, we nourish the spirit. And it is from our spirit which we become happy. Things don't bring us happiness. Material objects may make us comfortable or keep us entertained, but that does not account for any long-term happiness. If it did, then why are so many wealthy people helping to maintain the business of counseling and psychiatry? And why do some of the poorest people in the world appear to be so happy? So what is meditation, and how does it relate to disc golf?

Many people picture meditation involving a yogi sitting on a mountain chanting "Ommmm" repeatedly to achieve enlightenment. Or they see meditation as some weird, new age hippy activity. But meditation is not necessarily either of these things. Meditation does not have to be a posture or a religious experience. In its purest form, meditation is an ongoing process in our mind where we try to remain focused in a world where we are constantly barraged with distraction. Our jobs, bills, family problems, money... All of these things are on a constant tape loop in our mind, making it really difficult to focus on the things that really matter: such as our mental, physical, and spiritual health and in return, the excellent quality fruit we might be able to give to others. Meditation is taking the time to nourish our spirit. This, in most cases, involves releasing these distractions from our mind and focusing on one single thing. For the disc golfer, this one thing is: get this disc in that basket.

If you have ever carried a bunch of negative energy with you on the course, you know how it affects your game. If you had an argument with your girlfriend or boyfriend and are holding onto some form of anger or resentment while trying to play a round, you will discover that your game will suffer. You will miss easy drives and putts, and missing a shot will anger you more than it would if you were just out there having fun. Leaving your baggage in your vehicle is the is the first step in maintaining focus on what is essential at this moment: getting this disc in that basket. The practice of developing this focus and trimming away the excess negativity or distraction is the essence of meditation. It is that simple.

When we are able to watch our thoughts and how they affect us on an authentic plane, such as the disc golf course, it becomes easy to see how they are changing our lives, even if we aren't actively aware.

If you know anything about psychology, you know that one of the first places a psychologist is going to start looking when trying to identify the root of a person's problem is that person's childhood. They will try to bring out feelings and emotions you have been harboring for years, and usually, people have no idea that something that happened 20-some years ago is affecting their lives today. Then a psychologist will begin the process of helping them let it go of it piece by piece through various therapeutic techniques.

But imagine if you were well practiced at letting negative energy or emotions go as they occur in your life. The diffusion process would be much less painful and drawn out, and the negativity wouldn't have to affect you for the next 20 years.

To do this, we must first have an awareness of our thoughts and emotions. Then we need to learn to release negative thinking and feelings as they occur because carrying them around with us is unhealthy and unproductive. We must take time for ourselves to learn to focus on what really matters and trim away what doesn't. And we must nourish our spirit so that we can grow the fruit of happiness for ourselves and to share it with others.

If you carry your baggage with you on the course, you won't make great shots. You will see only the negative. You will be angry with your round, and you will walk off the course worse than ever. What is the point then?

So, leave your baggage in the car. It will not help you play a better round. It is only a distraction. Take time to play the game you love. Enjoy the possibility of every throw being a good one, and walk off the course generally feeling better than when you started. This is meditation. It is a process that takes work and will not happen on its own. It is an active process you have to be involved with personally.

This can also be likened to your disc golf bag. Any seasoned player knows that he is much more likely to make a given shot when his bag is placed firmly on the ground, and full concentration is given to the shot rather than quickly lobbing

MANY SHOTS ARE MISSED IN LIFE BECAUSE WE FAIL TO DROP OUR BAGGAGE AND GIVE FULL CONCENTRATION TO OUR TRUE GOALS.

the disc with his bag on his shoulder. No matter how close you are to the basket, you should always drop your bag, or hand full of discs, and give full attention. Many short putts are missed because a player is in a hurry and fails to drop his bag. I've seen pros do this in tournaments. Many shots are missed in life because we fail to drop our baggage and give full concentration to our goals.

What baggage do you carry around in your everyday life that is not creating a better you? Sometimes it is not easy to even notice that we have become weighed down with worrying about things that we cannot control or the thoughts of what someone else might think about us. Worry is a human problem. Animals don't worry, plants don't worry, but humans spend our lives worrying. Remember this: worry is praying for or visualizing what you don't want to happen. The questions you should always be asking yourself are: "Is this type of thinking or worry making me a better person?" and "Is this story I believe about me doing any good for me in the long run?"

If it is not, then I challenge you to change your focus to thoughts that do make you a better person. Because only when you remove your baggage can you truly be happy. Remember the old lobster cliche: A lobster in a pot of water doesn't know he's being boiled alive until it is too late. And remember, whether you are happy or not, you pass your emotions on to the people around you. Attitudes are contagious, good ones and bad ones.

A WALK IN THE WOODS
WITH A PURPOSE

"If you don't program yourself, life will program you."
- Les Brown

I often describe disc golf as "A walk in the woods with a purpose." This has to be the most basic way one can explain the game. Disc golf, in this way, is like no other sport.

Not many sports can be played alone, in the woods or in the fields, where a man (or a woman) can be alone with his or her thoughts. Or better yet, without them. Many times your thoughts about the world beyond the disc golf course are best left at home. Thoughts that are not directly related to getting your disc in the basket generally do not improve your game at all. "The purpose" should be the only thing guiding your mind, body, and spirit for the hour or two it takes to play a round of disc golf. "The purpose," your purpose on the course, should always be this: get this disc in that basket.

If you are busy thinking about everything else but your purpose, your strokes will begin to add up quickly and lead you to frustration. It takes a centered and focused mind to excel in the sport of disc golf. If you are thinking about the bills you have to pay while driving off the tee, your drive will certainly fail to go where you did not plan. If you are trying to make a putt while thinking about an argument you had with a family member before heading to the course, you will miss the chains.

But here's the catch - if you are thinking too hard about the drive you are trying to make, where your feet should be, how your shoulders are angled, how tight your grip should be, your drive will also fail. The trick then is to allow your body to do what you have trained it to do in practice and think only of your purpose - getting the disc in your hand into the basket on the horizon.

When looked at from this angle, disc golf becomes very similar to a walking meditation. It is actively monitoring your thinking. In a walking meditation, your focus is on walking, and nothing else. All we add here is the additional practice of throwing and reaching a goal. Your mind should be centered on that alone. Everything else in the world becomes indistinguishable noise (distraction), and you become one with the game.

What better way to clear your mind than to be alone, surrounded by nature, with a single and straightforward thought: Put this disc in that basket. When the task is completed, move on to the next hole and start again, leaving the last hole behind you. This is "the purpose" in its purest form. In meditation, the goal is to clear your mind. It is with a clear mind that disc golf can help one achieve vast human potential on this plane of existence.

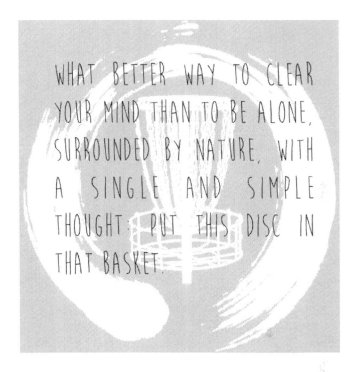

WHAT BETTER WAY TO CLEAR YOUR MIND THAN TO BE ALONE, SURROUNDED BY NATURE, WITH A SINGLE AND SIMPLE THOUGHT: PUT THIS DISC IN THAT BASKET.

Once you learn that all thinking not related to your purpose only hinders your game, the easier it will be for you to leave unrelated thoughts off the course. Being able to set this thinking or baggage aside for your game is not always the most natural thing to do and takes practice in itself, but it will become more comfortable with time.

Most people never lay their baggage down for anything. They carry this baggage with them everywhere they go, not noticing how much it holds them back in life. They enter into relationships carrying old relationship baggage and do not understand why their relationships always go wrong. They start new jobs with old work baggage and forever hate where they work. And if they do not practice laying their baggage aside for "their purpose," whatever their life's real purpose is, they will never truly reach their goals.

Lay your baggage aside and define your purpose. You may have many purposes, at home you have one purpose and at work another. Think about what you want. On the disc golf course, it is a low score or a perfect drive. What is it that you genuinely wish to have at home or at work? And what commitment will you make to yourself to gain it? The action of answering both of these questions as simply as possible will give you your "purpose." You may want to write it down so you can see it daily, then when you begin to stress over trivial matters, you will notice it quickly, reflect and move on. Are the things or people that stress you out carrying you towards "your purpose" or away from it? What changes in your life can you make and what mental baggage can you drop to assure that you meet your goals?

If you are able to do this and give full concentration to "your purpose," your game will improve, and you will enjoy your "walk in the woods" much more. Not only will your game improve, but you will notice more of the important things in life around you since your vision isn't completely clouded by the unnecessary. Once practiced, you will begin to notice how thoughts surface in your mind day to day, and if they do not benefit you, your goal or your purpose in life, you will be able to let them go. This is true meditation.

Zen in disc golf is to just throw the disc. Don't get bogged down with too much thinking. Allow yourself to just throw.

RIGHT ATTITUDE AND RIGHT FOCUS

"Staying focused is key when it comes to winning."
- **Nikko Locastro**

An unwavering, winning attitude, in combination with laser-like focus, will drastically improve any round of disc golf. These two mental strengths, positive attitude, and quality focus make up the most important psychological aspects of the game. I suppose they make up the most critical elements of any sport and definitely make up the two most vital mental aspects of day to day life. Attitude is the foundation of your focus, and it can make or break your game just as it can make or break your day. With the wrong attitude, you begin to lose focus. Without focus, your strokes will add up exponentially. Your ability to stay focused on the disc golf course relies on your ability to maintain a proper and positive mental attitude.

Your attitude is how you carry yourself, and it can have opposing extremes that can either influence or kill your game. Are you self-confident or self-doubting on the course? Are you humble or arrogant? Can you take a lousy stroke in stride and move on, or do you give into emotions too quickly and throw your bag when things don't go your way? Each extreme carries with it the ability to either make or destroy your game through the cultivation or destruction of your focus.

Additionally, more so than any other mental attribute involved in disc golf, attitude is the most contagious. And your attitude can be a positive influence on those around you, or it can be a cancer that affects everyone you surround yourself with. With the correct attitude, a player can create a focus that will reduce their scores beyond belief. The cultivation of a proper attitude relies on your ability to be a witness to your own self-talk. You must be able to listen to your thoughts, trimming away all negative self-talk, and nurture positive thinking. Only after building a strong foundation of positive attitude can you improve your focus.

Focus is an internal communication between your conscious self and sub-conscious self that allows you to throw farther, sink putts, and develop incredible accuracy that without focus would simply be unattainable. When entirely focused, a player does not over think a shot and "psych themselves out." They play their shot with unwavering confidence and trust in their ability that they have practiced the physical aspect of the game enough that their subconscious can take full control over their muscle memory. This allows the body to do what it has been trained to do without the risk of over thinking any particular shot. The goal of focus is to eliminate doubt. Doubt is the unseen killer of most people's game. Any shot you take, you must believe you will make. If you have already decided you will never make a particular shot or ace a specific hole, you never will, period. This is why a positive mental attitude (or P.M.A.) sets up the foundation for proper focus.

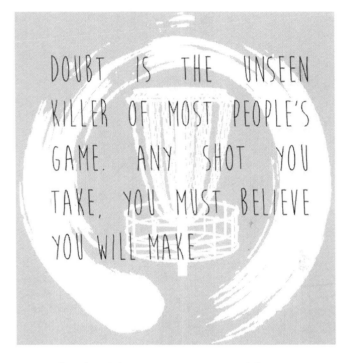

DOUBT IS THE UNSEEN KILLER OF MOST PEOPLE'S GAME. ANY SHOT YOU TAKE, YOU MUST BELIEVE YOU WILL MAKE.

Focus is also the ability to tune out external forces, pressures, onlookers, noise, weather, and even objects within your view that you find distracting. With accurate focus, you have your eye on the prize; you have an unwavering belief in yourself, and nothing internal or external will shake your ability to achieve your goal.

Imagine yourself standing 20 feet from a basket. You have

your favorite putter in your hand. You feel the grip of the disc and its weight. Now, with proper focus, the only thought that should be on your mind is "I CAN sink this putt." You list all the reasons you KNOW you can make it. "I have made many putts just like this. I have been playing well today. Everything seems right." You let your muscle memory do all the work without overthinking about technique. You have trained it over and over again in practice to sink this type of putt. You lock your vision on the pole or link in the chain, you pull back, release, watch its smooth flight, and hear the chains rattle. Perfect. With this attitude and focus, you are much more likely to hear chains ring than not.

Now imagine yourself standing in the same place, but instead, you tell yourself, "I don't know if I'll make this putt or not." Then you list all the reasons you don't believe in yourself. "I have missed my last few putts. I'm already several strokes up. So and so is playing better than me today. It seems like the wind is picking up." You have already talked yourself out of your ability to make your shot. You have lost your focus because you have removed the foundation of positive mental attitude from beneath its feet. You will miss every time. If you want to make your shot, you must believe that it is possible and that you can do it. In this way, focus is similar to having faith or confidence in your ability to achieve what you set your mind to do. It is said that a man with faith the size of a mustard seed can move a mountain. Indeed, with focus, faith, and confidence, you can sink more putts, and that is much easier than moving a whole mountain.

Several years ago, I was playing a pick-up game with two very different men. Both men were involved in the local disc golf club and were outstanding players. They both played in all the tournaments, but one of the men always placed in the top three while the other, who was just as experienced, placed well below him. The man who placed highest played with only one disc, an Innova Roc. He drove with it, did upshots with it, and putted with it and was one of the top players on the course. Throughout the day, he maintained a positive mental attitude even when his shots did not go as planned. He had amazing focus. He also was willing to help us out with our techniques and give us pointers.

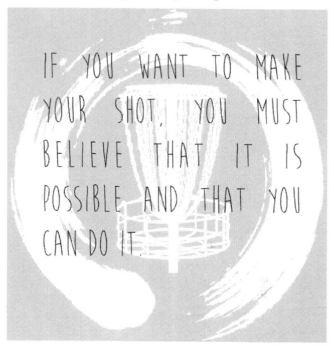

IF YOU WANT TO MAKE YOUR SHOT, YOU MUST BELIEVE THAT IT IS POSSIBLE AND THAT YOU CAN DO IT.

The other man played with a full bag and had the best flick shot I had ever seen, but his attitude was unbalanced. When he threw a great shot, he became arrogant and would go on and on about how great he was. When he hit a tree, he would throw his bag and get so angry that it really made everyone else feel awkward and uncomfortable. When his shots did not go his way, he blamed everything else in the world except himself. He'd say, "I hate this course. I hate this hole. These discs are too light. I need different discs!" After 9 holes, I was ready to stop playing with them because of this guy's attitude. The other gentleman did not say much about it. He was so focused that it did not interrupt his game. My focus, however, was interrupted as the man's attitude spread like a cancer. Because he was so easily frustrated, the rest of us got quickly frustrated. His attitude had become so infectious that it was killing our focus and our games, too. But the other man who maintained a positive mental attitude continued playing, birdying hole after hole with his beat up old Roc. This man continued to play well because he never lost focus, and that's why he was one of the top pros on the course.

Once you practice the proper attitude and focus for a long enough time, you build it into a fortress that does not allow self-doubt and frustration in, yours or anyone else's. Those elements of distraction and negativity that used to attack your foundation and seemed like giant cannonballs being fired upon a decrepit wooden shack, now they look like tiny arrows hitting the walls of your well constructed and sturdy castle. Building attitude and focus takes just as much practice as building muscle memory and learning to throw your discs consistently and adequately. To build them, a player must notice negativity, distractions, and self-doubt building within their mind then quickly adjust their mindset with positive thinking and self-confident thoughts. Noticing negative self-talk and distraction means paying attention. It means being in the moment.

Without proper mental practice, you will never build your castle of positive attitude and laser-like focus. It is imperative that you work on these psychological aspects of your game just as hard as the physical ones if you want to see your scores dramatically lowered. The good thing is that you don't have to be on the course to practice these skills. These skills, like many other skills, are just as much about who you are off the course as who you are on the course.

When you go to work, do you go in with confidence or with self-doubt? Do you go in with humbleness or arrogance? These traits are transmitted with you through your words, your body language, and your work. I guarantee you that you will attract more abundance in your day to day life if you walk with confidence, with humbleness, and with focus than if you allow negative thinking to control your life. These things will show in how you carry yourself. Your co-workers will notice, your boss will notice, and your clients will notice.

Many people give themselves like the easily frustrated man, arrogant when they achieve and ticking time-bombs when things don't go as planned. They spend the majority of their day pointing fingers at everything and everyone else for the bad things that happen in their lives. They blame the company they work for just as the man accused the holes. They hate their job and rationalize that the grass is greener elsewhere as the man blamed the disc golf course. And they act as if the entire world is out to get them as the man accused the wind and the trees. They throw blame all around, never taking a look at themselves and their attitude, while everyone around them continues to play their game and improve.

The key for you is not to fall into this bottomless pit of poor attitude but to continue to stay focused and just play the game, keeping your eyes on your goals. Believe in yourself at work as you believe in your ability to make putts. In the long run, just as the negative man's strokes added up on the course, these people in your life with negative mental attitudes will dig their own graves while you continue to excel. It is imperative that you do not fall into the trap of grave digging with them.

Do not get upset or frustrated when things do not go your way in life or on the course; just find your disc, pitch back in, and play on. Remember, that's why golf is played on 18 holes and not only 1. When we find ourselves in a difficult situation on one hole, we have 17 more holes where we can make it up, provided we keep a stable positive mental attitude. Learn from your mistakes and move on. With the right attitude and the proper focus, no setback will ever stand between you and your prize. If you believe in yourself and do not let outside forces distract you, then nothing can keep you down.

One more thing I'd like to point out about these two men is that the man who always placed in the top three took time to help others with their techniques, while the easily frustrated man took no time at all because he was too busy being either arrogant or angry. The man who took the time to help us recognized that his investment in others was an investment in himself. When we take time and energy to teach others, we realize how much we know, and we find that the energy is returned back to us with interest.

THE SECRET FORMULA FOR SUCCESS

"It's the mental mistakes that cost you wins."
- **Paul McBeth**

We've already talked about the importance of the three aspects of a balanced game and a balanced life. We've talked about the physical side of the game, and how anything we want to be good at in life we must practice. We have talked about the mental side of the game and how important focus and attitude is in improving your game and your life. And last but not least, we have talked about the spiritual side of the game and how the game helps us to reflect on who we are as players and who we are as people.

Now I'd like to talk about what I call the "formula for success." This formula works on and off the disc golf course, and it fully encompasses the three aspects of balance. The formula is simple:

DESIRE + BELIEF + PERSISTENCE = SUCCESS

As with all previous topics, we will take a look at how this formula works on the disc golf course, and then we will take a look at how it relates to life.

Let's break down the elements of the formula beginning with the word success.

What is success? If you ask 10 people what the word success means, you will most likely get 10 different answers, but if you're standing on a tee pad, then you know what success means at that particular moment. Success from the tee pad means getting your disc in the basket in or under par. And if that is your definition of success on the tee pad, then you have mentally defined your desire. Success is the achievement of your desire.

Most of us never think about it, but as soon as we step on the tee pad and see the hole that we're about to tee off on, we already have an ideal number of strokes in mind. A number that we believe is acceptable to get us from the tee to the basket for us to feel successful. That number in our mind is derived very quickly and comes from several different factors other than just the par number on the sign. The first is our idea of how difficult we believe that hole will be. If we have a visual on the basket, see very few obstacles, and know that we can throw that distance with accuracy, then we choose, in our mind, a very low acceptable number for success. The second factor that determines this number is our competitive goal. For example, if we know that we are one stroke above the competition and need to lower our score by a stroke, we may use that when we determine the acceptable number for a successful score on that hole. The third factor might be how well we've played that hole in the past. In this example, if we generally par the hole, then we know that a par or birdie would be successful and a bogie would be less than successful for us.

So as we step up to the tee pad, we have outlined our desire in our mind. We have already defined what we consider to be a success. In such a case, desire is the mental part of the formula.

The second part of the formula for success is belief or faith. And by belief or faith, I mean the confidence in yourself that the achievement of your desire is possible. This means when you step up on the tee pad that you have no doubt that what you desire is possible, that you are able to park a shot underneath the basket for a birdie or that you are actually able even to ace the hole. The achievement of your desire weighs heavily on your belief of its possibility. If every time you step up on the tee pad, you say to yourself, "I've never made a birdie on this hole before; I most likely will never make a birdie," the chances of you making that birdie or any other birdie are slim to none and are left to sheer luck. But if you step up to the tee pad with the defined desired that you want to make a birdie and that you know it's possible then your chances of making that birdie go up exponentially. Faith and belief are the spiritual part of the success formula.

The last part of the formula is persistence. You have already defined your desire in your mind; you know what it means to be successful. And in addition to understanding what your desire is, you believe that it's possible to achieve it. The final part of the equation is persistence; that is never to stop trying to fulfill your desire. In this way, you will be successful. Persistence is the physical part of the formula.

Each of these elements in the formula for success is dependent on the other two; you cannot add up only two of these elements to equal success without relying heavily on luck. Let's take a look at what that means.

If you cannot define success, then you cannot be successful; to define success, you must know what your desire is. Without a defined desire, there is no defined success. Most successful people state their first step to success is writing down their goals or desires.

If you know what your desire is and you continue to practice physically but do not believe in yourself, then you are missing the element of belief, and if you are missing the element of belief, it is extremely difficult to be successful. You must believe that you can achieve.

You can have all of the desire in the world and all of the belief that you can achieve that desire but if you do not physically practice with persistence, inevitably you never put it into action, or you quit on yourself before you can become successful.

On the disc golf course, this means knowing what your goals are. If your goal is to shoot six under par, then achievement of that goal would be a success. You have defined your desire by knowing what your goal is. The next step is to believe that you can shoot that six under par and then follow up by never quitting until you achieve that goal.

Off the disc golf course, this formula works the exact same way: knowing what your goals are (and I suggest writing them down) - believing in yourself that you can achieve your goals and finally, persisting until your goals have been achieved. If you consistently follow this formula, you have done everything in your power to achieve success.

ALL OBSTACLES
LEAD TO GROWTH

"Try not to overreact to a bad shot. It's only one shot out of however many you may take. If you take the anger from the bad shot with you it will affect the next throw and the next one until eventually you are in a downward spiral."

- Liz Carr

Playing a good round disc golf relies on your ability to get over, past, and around obstacles such as trees, bushes, lakes, etc. Without obstacles, the game would be boring. Naturally, as disc golfers, we always want to try to create that nice clear shot at the basket, but it is the nature of the game that makes these easy shots so elusive. And rightly so, games are about challenge. Subtract challenge from a game, and it ceases to be a game and becomes just another mindless task. This is what helps you to develop your skills in all different types of shots, from hyzers to anhyzers, from scoobies to turbo putts. It also creates the need for different kinds of discs with varying types of flight patterns.

Since obstacles "make up the game," and it would be preposterous to believe that you'll never hit a tree, find a bad lie, or lose your disc in a lake at some time. I often tell people, "You aren't playing disc golf if you haven't hit a tree," or "If you haven't lost a disc…you haven't been playing long enough." These things are just facts of life on the course, and we all know this, but what separates a great player from a regular guy lobbing discs every which way in the woods is how they perceive these obstacles.

If you hit a tree, do you get mad and let your anger ruin the rest of the hole for you? Or do you merely take it in stride, laugh it off, allow it to motivate you to focus harder, and make each shot as a new beginning? It's critical not to let one or even ten bad throws ruin the rest of your game. If you want to keep a low score, you must view each shot as a new chance to get closer to or into the basket. Overthinking about a past shot will only erode your attitude and focus. Every shot must be made on its own. Never allow a few poor throws to ruin your whole outlook and the rest of your game. You must let yourself to hit some trees, to have some wild throws, and to lose a disc every now and then. Making mistakes in disc golf does not say nearly as much about how good a player you are as how you can pick up your disc and move on. This is called resilience, and it is imperative that you develop a tremendous amount of resilience to play a superior game.

In fact, hitting a tree and finding a poor lie only makes you a better player. It forces you to play it where it lies. It forces you to develop an arsenal of shots and skills you may have never developed if you did not occasionally find yourself in a bad situation. It forces you to build resilience, a characteristic that is not only imperative in disc golf but in survival as well. Next time you hit a tree right off the tee and begin to beat yourself up, remind yourself, even professional players hit trees (all the time!). Hitting a few trees is not what separates a recreational player from becoming a pro. What separates a recreational player from a pro is what the pro does next.

We all face obstacles in daily life. But it is not these obstacles that define our character; it is how we choose to see these obstacles, how we react to them, and how we adapt to survive despite them that defines our character. The obstacles we hit in life often help us to build on our ability to adjust and show resilience. Some personal growth may be possible from reading books on resilience or watching YouTube videos on building confidence, and not making your own personal mistakes, but with the proper mindset, mistakes bring quality growth that does not merely wither with time but will endure for the long haul.

The best story of resilience and proper mindset on and off the course I can think of is that of my good friend, Don Dixon, who broke his arm playing disc golf by throwing a shot a little too close to a tree. Don was in a cast and a sling for the next 4-6 months. Don is also one of the only DG players I have ever met who may be more passionate about the sport than I am. For most people, an injury like that would mean that he would be out of the game for the coming months, but not for Don. He took it upon himself to set up his portable basket in his backyard and slowly began teaching himself how to putt left-handed. As time moved on, he gradually learned how to drive left-handed as well. When the cast came off, after a few months of rehabilitation of his right arm, Don was now an ambidextrous player, which gave him a considerable leap up on the game. Before the break, Don could not throw left-handed at all, but after the break, he routinely beats me round after round. Long story short: Don hit a tree, and now he is a better player.

Most people I meet don't seem to have this attitude on the course or in life. They allow obstacles to get them down. They let a few poor shots to ruin their game or even their day. Often I tell people who are beating themselves up about a weak shot on the course: "That's why they make 18 holes."

It is not important how many obstacles you hit. What is important is what you do next.

EVERY STROKE IS IMPORTANT

*"Even simple shots...are just as important as a big drive or a long putt.
Both require [...] a mind that is in the moment."*
- **Steven Jacobs**

It is immensely important to understand that in disc golf,
every stroke is important; therefore each type of throw must
be practiced to develop and maintain a balanced game.

The importance of the practice of individual skills can never
be understated, but for you to see results in your scorecard,
all elements must come together to result in a balanced game.
The drive is no more or no less important than the putt. The
putt is no more or less crucial than the drive. And the upshot
is no more or less important than the drive or the putt.
Because a player must be proficient in all aspects of the
game, he must also balance all elements of practice.

Many times, players become obsessed with their driving
distance and spend 80 to 90 percent of their time practicing

drives to gain more distance, and their putting suffers. Unfortunately, this is not noticed during practice but during a game or tournament setting, so later they head back to the drawing board and begin to spend 80 to 90 percent of their time practicing putting. As a result, their drives suffer. Either way, if they cannot maintain a balanced game, their score will not improve.

An overconfident player may sacrifice his game by not tuning into himself for full focus in every shot, whether it's a 300-foot drive or 2-foot putt. All strokes count; therefore, all strokes are equally important. Many putts are missed in tournaments due to a player's lackadaisical attitude, which can cause him to miss even the shortest of putts because he has not given himself a chance to gain focus.

There can be a fine line between confidence and arrogance on the disc golf course. No matter how short the putt, a player must have his mind on the shot. Many times a player may believe that his upshot was so good and put him so close that he does not have to have stay focused for a short putt. Also, a player may also have his mind on his next tee-shot and not place his bag down for a tap-in putt, which may restrict his throw and cause him to miss. Your mind must be in the moment for every shot, not thinking about a past shot and not thinking about a future shot.

On the scorecard, all shots are weighed the same and counted as a single stroke. In some ways, a missed short putt is more painful than a bad drive. To achieve a good round of disc golf, a player must balance his practice with all types of shots and also have his mind in the game at all times.

This is just as in life. To achieve true wholeness, we must maintain a balanced lifestyle, a balanced diet, a balanced exercise routine, and balanced work and family life. In addition to a balanced lifestyle, a person who is mindful in every moment will be able to experience the abundant joys that life has to offer, which may be difficult if not impossible to achieve if one has his mind always in the past or in the future.

Just as every stroke in disc golf is important, every moment in life is important. Therefore one should live always practicing mindfulness, thought observation, and awareness of the now and to attempt to achieve balance in their life.

TRAIN HOW YOU PLAY
PLAY HOW YOU TRAIN

"My tip would be PRACTICE, you can't improve without it. Good practice makes good play, Sloppy practice makes sloppy play."
- Paul McBeth

Eleven years ago, I started my career as a Medic Firefighter for a city on the east coast of Virginia. After I was hired, 15 other recruits and I went through a grueling and rigorous training academy. One of our mottos in the fire academy was "Train how you fight, and fight how you train." This means developing habits on the training ground that we would hopefully replicate during actual incidents without thinking about them. Stressful incidents I might add. These habits included always wearing our firefighting gear correctly, always checking off our equipment appropriately, and NEVER letting go of that nozzle. If we missed the smallest detail in any exercise, punishment ensued. I did more push-ups in my fire academy than I had ever done my entire life. At the time, these punishments seemed excessive, but I can honestly tell you that as a firefighter, learning attention to detail saves

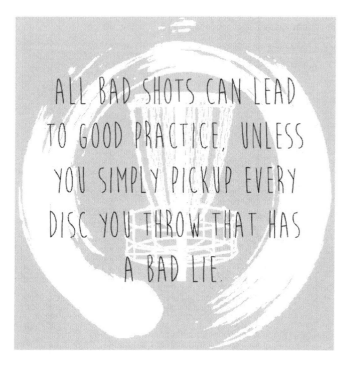

ALL BAD SHOTS CAN LEAD TO GOOD PRACTICE, UNLESS YOU SIMPLY PICKUP EVERY DISC YOU THROW THAT HAS A BAD LIE.

people's lives. I am sure that it has saved mine already in many situations I have been in on the job.

Learning how to train how you fight takes some imagination. In my firefighter training, there were often no flames licking at our helmets, but we acted like there were about to be some any moment.

On the disc golf course, when we are out just playing for fun or playing practice rounds, there is no judge around. We can always throw another mulligan, we can foot fault off the tee pad, and we can merely tap the chains with our disc after a close upshot. But I ask you, how does this really benefit us in the long run?

Of course, throwing a mulligan off the tee gives you another shot at practicing a drive, but if you simply pick up your disc every time it has a bad lie, how do you ever practice getting yourself out of trouble? All bad shots can lead to good practice unless you simply pick up every disc you throw that has a bad lie. Drives can be practiced in field time. Using bad lies on the course can only improve your disc golfing abilities, by helping you to become a more well-rounded player.

If you pick up your disc on every bad shot, you have shorted yourself later when you find your disc with a lousy lie during a tournament and can't figure out how to pitch it back in. When you need that forehand shot or turbo putt, will you be able to pull it out of your bag of tricks and use it successfully?

Similarly, allowing yourself and your group to bend the rules during a practice match only creates terrible habits on the disc golf course. If you don't make foot-faults a big deal in practice, you will foot fault in a tournament. If you tap your disc in at the basket and do not physically drop it in, you will do this in a tournament also, and you will be penalized.

If you always practice how you play, you will have a better and more realistic experience during tournament play. You will perform how you have practiced. You will not have built up bad habits, and you will be able to trust yourself to get out of dangerous situations.

This is not to say take your game so seriously that you do not have fun on the course, but hold yourself accountable relative to the seriousness you feel for the game. Being a stickler and developing good habits in practice will reflect when your score really matters. Paying attention to detail will always pay back higher returns than allowing yourself to slip out of laziness.

Every shot in your bag must be so practiced that under additional stress, all your physical training can take over so that all you will need to be concerned about is allowing your mind to focus.

In life and in business, an ethical person is one who does the right thing even when no one is looking. And if you always do the right thing you can never be wrong. In the short run, you may be viewed as someone who takes life too seriously, but in the long term, you will be better able to handle anything that happens in your life. If you have paid attention to detail in practice and have also practiced getting yourself out of tight spots, you will be able to trust yourself to show resilience at the moment when it really matters. You will not falter, you will thrive.

THE POWER OF
VISUALIZATION

"It has proved successful when I could already picture the disc going into the basket moments before actually making that putt, when you can envision it happening, it will happen."
-Avery Jenkins

"The human mind is tricky and 'don't throw in the water', is the same as 'please, let's throw in the water now'."
- Erik Smith

Few activities, aside from persistent practice, can increase your ability to be successful on the disc golf course than visualization. Visualization is the act of seeing your shot before it is made. The ability to visualize will dramatically lower your score and take your game to unimaginable heights, but to do this correctly a player must have a solid foundation of positive attitude and proper focus. Only when a player has a self-confident attitude and the ability to tune

VISUALIZE SECOND FOR SECOND THE AMOUNT OF TIME YOUR DISC WILL BE IN THE AIR. NO MORE. NO LESS.

out all distraction, will genuinely game enhancing visualization occur.

Every shot you take you should be able to imagine exactly where the shot should land, how it should fly, how it should feel leaving your hand. Take 5 to 10 seconds before making each shot to do this, and I guarantee you will watch your bogies become pars, your pars become birdies, and your birdies become aces.

When you step up on the tee box, after selecting a path for the flight of your disc, a disc that you know will take that flight path, and the type of throw you want to use, do not just lob the disc without first drawing in your focus and visualizing every aspect of your shot.

Never rush your throw. Many throws go wrong when a player feels rushed. This shows that the player has lost focus and feels hurried either because of distracting internal forces or outside pressures on him. Recognize that feeling rushed is all in your mind. According to the PDGA rulebook, you have 30 seconds to throw, use that time to see every aspect of your disc's flight. Stand where you will be throwing. Draw your focus in, tuning out all other thoughts. Step inside your psyche and visualize your shot like a movie playing in your mind. Mentally feel the disc leave your hand, watching it fly through the air and navigate around trees and obstacles, see it land, roll, or skip to your desired location. The rule I use is to visualize second for second the amount of time your disc will be in the air. No more. No less.

On your upshot follow the same instructions. Draw in focus. Visualize the shot and do not release until you have fully watched the video play in your mind of your disc landing mere feet or inches from your target.

Visualizing your putt going into the basket is the best thing that will ever happen to your short game because the putt is not about power as much as it is about accuracy. First, believe you can make your putt. Next, build on that belief by focusing and shutting out all inside voices telling you what your score is or how important that particular putt will be for your round. Shut out all outside noise and really draw your focus into the pole or link in the chain you desire to hit. Now visualize the disc leaving your hand again and heading straight for that focus point. Get all the applicable senses you can into your visualization. Hear the rattling of the chains in your mind, and feel the excitement of making your putt, and take it even one step further by seeing and hearing everyone in your group say "great shot!"

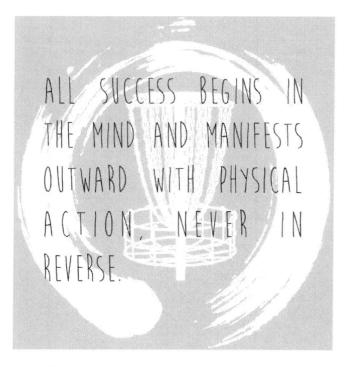

ALL SUCCESS BEGINS IN THE MIND AND MANIFESTS OUTWARD WITH PHYSICAL ACTION, NEVER IN REVERSE.

Do all of this before your disc leaves your hand. It only takes 5 to 10 seconds and will improve your game dramatically. Scientific studies are now showing that the time spent visualizing does a person seven times greater good than time spent in actual physical practice. This means that if you spend an hour playing a round of disc golf visualizing every shot, you have increased your ability more than if you were to have spent 7 hours practicing only the physical aspects of your game.

Think about it, how many times have you stepped up and hurled a horrible shot into the woods only to say to yourself "take your time next time!" What does this self-instruction mean, "take your time?" If you took your time, what would you "take your time" doing? The best players know that "taking your time" means allowing yourself enough time to draw in your focus and to visualize your shots before you make them.

The same fact remains true in any activity you do. And everything done with prior visualization will become dramatically more successful than rushing into anything. Rushing into jobs, relationships, and investments never seem to work out better than if you take your time to visualize all possible outcomes, or better yet the results you want for yourself. All success begins in the mind and manifests outward with physical action, never in reverse.

Some of the greatest athletes of all time have utilized visualization to propel their athleticism to great heights. Olympic athletes spend years practicing visualization, many times practicing visualizing their entire Olympic event, from the moment it begins to the time they are given their gold medals. One of the United States Olympic Team's sports psychologists, Nicole Detling, stated: "The more an athlete can image the entire package, the better it's going to be." Golfer, Jack Nicklaus is the 3rd highest winning PGA Tour member and has been quoted saying he never takes a shot without visualizing every aspect of its flight or roll. Marc McGuire says before stepping up to bat that he visualizes pitches before they happen.

Not only athletes utilize visualization. The most successful people to have ever lived from businessmen to entertainers all praise the act of visualization and credit it for their successes. From Ansel Adams to Albert Einstein, Nikola Tesla to Shakespeare, Curtis Strange to Jim Carrey, the most successful people believe success begins in the mind.

COMING OFF
AUTO-PILOT

"One main difference between Pro and Ams is that Ams are unable to correct flaws in their technique but Pros are able to correct any faults on the very next throw instead of letting it affect them the rest of the round."

-Avery Jenkins

Every round of disc golf is different. It is the nature of the sport. Even if you are only playing your home course, you will find many nuances that change gameplay, from varying degrees of wind to seasons and foliage (or lack of). Even temperature can change your disc flight because discs soften in the heat and harden in the cold. There are no "average days" on the course.

The course changes, the conditions change, your tools change, and your competition changes. Therefore, to win, you must adapt and change with the conditions. If you

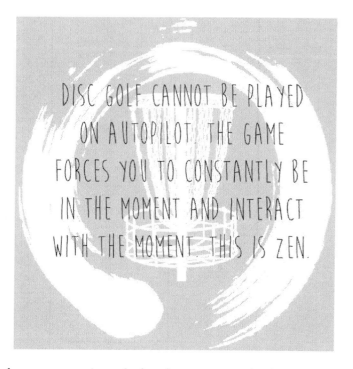

DISC GOLF CANNOT BE PLAYED ON AUTOPILOT. THE GAME FORCES YOU TO CONSTANTLY BE IN THE MOMENT AND INTERACT WITH THE MOMENT. THIS IS ZEN.

always stay static and play the game exactly the same way every day, you set yourself up for failure. A champion knows that the one thing that must remain constant is focus in the face of adversity, and as we discussed earlier - adversity is not your enemy. Adversity makes you a stronger player. It forces you to adjust and be resilient. Adversity is your friend.

You may start the round out grabbing your go-to discs, only to realize they just aren't working that day. The definition of insanity is continuing to do the same thing over and over and expecting the results to change. You must continually experiment to force your game to meet the needs of the conditions in front of you. This is how a player creates mastery.

You may begin a round conservatively, keeping your shots short and accurate only to realize that your competition is making greater stride taking higher risks and throwing long. The assessment of what is working and what is not is critical. Disc golf cannot be played on auto-pilot. The game forces you to be in the moment and interact with the moment continually.

This is also true in life. If you find yourself at work or at home creating "manufactured stress," it may be because your auto-pilot is taking you against the natural flow of the moment and against the grain of the optimal you. Being conscious of your constantly changing situations, conditions, and even competition will keep you in a heightened state of awareness that will help you assess if you are headed down the correct path or the wrong one.

Many of us walk into new and different situations in life grabbing the same old tools we have used over and over, just to find ourselves defeated and stressed out. And who is to blame? A co-worker? A relative? A boss? Or can we blame ourselves for not being in the state of mind to recognize that just like in disc golf, we need to continually assess our surroundings and situations, come off autopilot, and be able to mold ourselves and our tools - be it communication, body language, or even personal philosophies. We must study and train on these things to be successful in life, just as we practice backhand drives and forearm throws on the disc golf course.

Most of our problems in life are a result of being on auto-pilot. Being mindful means coming off that auto-pilot. Thought observation helps dismantle the ticking time bomb of your thinking patterns and attitudes, no longer letting them rule over you, but ruling over them. This is where success begins.

CHOOSING YOUR OPPONENTS

"All in all this is a great thing, with competition level increasing, it just means the sport is progressing in the correct direction! I'm excited for the future!"
- Eric McCabe

True growth on the disc golf course requires a combination of both inner and outer factors. We have thoroughly discussed the importance of strengthening the inner side of your game by conditioning your mind, body, and spirit to help you win, but to leave the conversation, there would be to imply that our growth only occurs from the inside-out without help from outside forces.

While it is true that a tree grows from the inside-out, it is also true that it must rely on external elements for its survival. Water, sunlight, and soil make it grow tall and strong. A tree also must withstand wind, rain, and extreme temperatures. Without all of these elements working together, it withers and dies.

The other players that you regularly play with are a significant aspect of your outside forces that will have a similar effect on your growth, stagnation, or even your decline in successful play.

Though it can be said that you are in competition mainly with yourself and the course, there is a competitive nature to the sport. A healthy competitive nature will without a doubt push you beyond the limits of only playing solo. A robust competitive nature helps you strive to improve, to have a clearer vision of your goals, and overall enjoy your time on the course through camaraderie.

This, of course, is juxtaposed with unhealthy competition in which yourself or other players take competitiveness to a level where those involved cannot have fun anymore. This category would include both "sore losers" and "sore winners." These types of players suck the fun out of the game, and if they have no further redeeming quality to enhance your growth, they should be avoided.

There are three types of players that you should play with on a consistent basis. They are your "Mentor Group," your "Peer Group," and your "Protege Group."

The first step to improving your game through competition is to select opponents that are just better than you. This forces you to rise to the challenge. These players may also have a lot of insight and experience, and if willing to be generous (as most are), they can share tips and secrets with you to help you with you to improve on the course. This group is your "Mentor group." A mentor is a wise and trusted guiding advisor. These players will assist in leading you on your path to success. If you never play with a mentor group, you miss out on a lot of advice and objective clarity that could be added to your game. You cannot see yourself

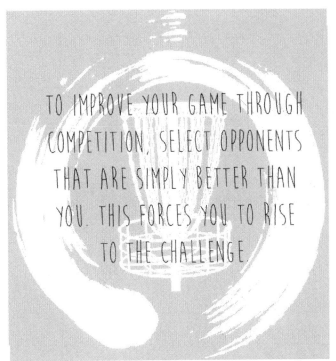

TO IMPROVE YOUR GAME THROUGH COMPETITION, SELECT OPPONENTS THAT ARE SIMPLY BETTER THAN YOU. THIS FORCES YOU TO RISE TO THE CHALLENGE.

throw a drive or a putt. But other members of your "mentor group" can and may be able to see what you are doing right or wrong. Find trusted players who can help you reach your goals. You should strive to play with your "Mentor group" frequently.

This group will be the sunlight on your tree and will help feed your success.

The next group you should play with is your "Peer Group." These are the players that play at the same level as you. Practice with these individuals what you have learned with your "Mentor Group." These players will help you remain grounded in the game. They can also provide benchmarks, showing you where your training and practice is taking you.

They also can help keep the game lighthearted and fun, provided they share your passion and positive attitude for the sport.

Your peer group will be the soil to your tree, grounding you and showing you how far you have come.

Lastly, the third group you should play with will be your "Protege Group." This is the group that YOU are mentoring, teaching, and training. They can be brand new players or players that have come to you, asking for your insight. Mentoring can be hugely rewarding as you: A) feel like you are helping someone else and B) realize how much you have grown from your time spent practicing and playing on the course. Over time these players will no doubt join your "Peer Group" with your advice and their practice. When this occurs, keep finding new players to mentor. I cannot tell you how gratifying it is to help others and become a witness to their growth. Never be afraid to share your knowledge with other people, feeling like it gives them a competitive advantage. Sharing your experience will improve your game at the same rate as it improves theirs because it forces you to pay attention and take yourself off auto-pilot while you break down what you are good at to assist others. And if by some chance they become better than you, pat yourself on the back because it was YOU that helped create a champion!

It is immensely important that you balance your time with these 3 different groups. Sacrifice any of them, and your game will no doubt begin to slip due to flaws in our basic human psychology. Let me explain If you only play with your "Mentor Group" and consistently come in last, over time your mind will begin to make you believe you will never be as good as they are. The fun will run out, and you will no doubt play less frequently as you begin to feel defeated. Secondly, if you only play with your "Peer Group," you risk stagnation. You may not find areas to grow and may find

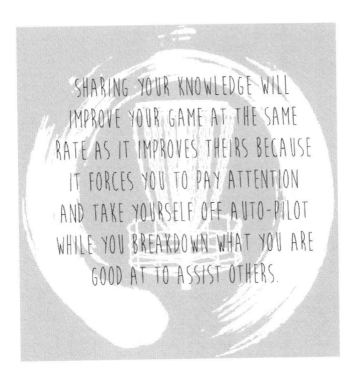

SHARING YOUR KNOWLEDGE WILL IMPROVE YOUR GAME AT THE SAME RATE AS IT IMPROVES THEIRS BECAUSE IT FORCES YOU TO PAY ATTENTION AND TAKE YOURSELF OFF AUTO-PILOT WHILE YOU BREAKDOWN WHAT YOU ARE GOOD AT TO ASSIST OTHERS.

yourself getting just plain bored. Thirdly, if you only play with your "Protege Group," you may lose patience, and you may get just plain lazy because you are only paying with a low level of competition. You must strike a balance.

Of course, these rules and groups apply off the course as well. If you want to be a real success story, you must be willing to surround yourself with people who are better than you or smarter than you at whatever you are striving to be successful at. The most successful men and women in history have known this, from Henry Ford to Steve Jobs. The fastest way to create success is to download the information great men have already done the hard work to learn for you. It is advisable that this real life "Mentor Group" be people you actually know, but if not possible, find greatness everywhere - from articles to books, and from radio to video. We are lucky to live in this information age that we can merely download others experiences from successes to mistakes at the click of a mouse button. It is unfortunate that many people do not see how wonderful this is. The answers are out there. You must just begin asking the questions.

You also need your "Peer Group," your friends, your family, the people who stay static in your life - through thick and thin. It's incredible to think that everything in my life could change for the worse tomorrow, and I have collected enough beautiful people who will ride it out with me regardless. This is love and a real army of power. Be grateful for this group because it keeps you grounded.

And nothing, I mean nothing brings more life satisfaction than improving the lives of the people around you. Your "Protege Group" whether it be a new co-worker, or your child, or even a stranger can be a constant source of happiness. As you openly give to others, the universe will readily give to you - but here is the catch YOU must be open to receive all the success and joy life as to offer.

AS YOU OPENLY GIVE TO OTHERS,
THE UNIVERSE WILL OPENLY GIVE
TO YOU - BUT HERES THE CATCH
YOU MUST BE OPEN TO RECEIVE
ALL THE SUCCESS AND JOY LIFE AS
TO OFFER.

KEEP THE PLAY IN *PLAYING*

"Play is the highest form of research."

- Albert Einstein

A wise man once said, "If you love what you do then you will never work a day in your life." I realize that for 99% of players, disc golf is not a money-making occupation (though how cool would it be?), but sometimes it's not the act of getting paid to do something that makes it work, it is how you are making yourself feel while you are doing it that makes it feel like "work."

The mindset you carry with you can dictate whether it has gone from a fun day on the course to feeling like it is "work." I met a player on the course one time whose favorite saying when someone asked how he was doing was "I am not at work, and I am not at home...I am doing great!" Of course, this may not speak much to his work or home life, but the fact is he had separated what he was doing on the course from being "work." For him, his time on the course is a mini-vacation.

IF DISC GOLF EVER BECOMES MORE STRESS THAN YOU CAN HANDLE, DROP YOUR DISCS AND GET OFF THE COURSE. YOU NEED TO RE-ALIGN YOUR MIND.

So what kind of mindset or attitude on the course makes playing the great game of disc golf "work?" Most people dislike where they work for several reasons: First, they dislike work because they don't find it stimulating. They go from day to day being bored and wondering if there is any meaning to what they are spending half their lives doing. Most disc golfers do not get bored playing disc golf, quite the opposite. The game of disc golf attracts people because (whether they know or understand it or not) it IS stimulating their mind, body, and spirit.

If disc golf has lost its appeal to you through boredom, change it up! Play different courses, different tees, different baskets. Find different opponents, different discs, different ways to see the game. This is such an easy fix, I personally don't believe that many disc golfers come to look at the game as "work" for this reason.

Secondly, people don't like where their jobs because they have TOO MUCH on their plate. In other words, work creates more stress for them than they would care to handle. If disc golf ever becomes more weight than you can manage, drop your discs and get off the course. You need to re-align your mind. You are taking the game too seriously and have made it not fun anymore. Reach back in time and recall the things that made the game so appealing to you. Come out again refreshed, ready to play. I believe disc golf is one of the most significant ways to relieve stress, if your game is stressing you out, your mind is not where you need to be.

Thirdly, people dislike "work" because they hate their co-workers. On the course, your co-workers are the people you are playing with. First of all, examine yourself to make sure your problem with them isn't a problem for you. If after reviewing yourself and you find that it really is them and not you, find a different group to play with. This is your time. Fire them, hire new opponents that lift you up and do not bring you down.

And lastly but most importantly people dislike "work" because they dislike their boss. On the course, you are your boss, and you are in full control of how hard you are on yourself when things don't go your way. It is a fact that most people are harder on themselves than any of their peers. Do you miss a putt and throw your bag? Do you yell, scream, or curse when your drive just isn't acting the way you want? It may be that your inner "boss" is being too hard on you. You have two options at this point: quit or fire your "inner boss." Disc golf should be fun. Whether you are playing with some buddies or in an official PDGA tournament when the fun leaves success follows.

You must be in the proper mindset to succeed and finding fault in everything including yourself takes the fun away and makes it "work." Even the top professionals can't be successful on the course if they are hating their job. When you feel like your game has become "work." You need to put your bag down and walk away until you can change your attitude. You will not improve with negative thinking.

This is also true off the course. Sometimes we all take things in life a little too seriously. And once we have done that, we have taken the fun out of whatever we are doing and have made it work. The secret is, you have to love what you do, no matter what you are doing. Sure, there are things that we all must do that we may not like to do. But if you can cultivate a positive attitude in one area of your life, then you can cultivate it in another. A positive attitude will make the most mundane tasks at least feel like they are getting done faster. A positive attitude clears the mind. A negative attitude clogs the mind. Both are contagious in all aspects of your life.

A POSITIVE ATTITUDE CLEARS THE MIND. A NEGATIVE ATTITUDE CLOGS THE MIND. BOTH ARE CONTAGIOUS IN ALL ASPECTS OF YOUR LIFE.

YOUR THOUGHTS
BECOME YOU

"I believe you need a plan on how to think, as well as how you intend to play the course. You simply can't be a victim of your bad shots or bad luck. A lot of players will dwell on a bad hole and carry negative thoughts onto later shots."
- Erik Smith

In chaos theory, there is a concept called the Butterfly Effect that hypothesizes that a butterfly flapping its wings in Brazil could cause a hurricane in Florida. There have also been experiments by physicist Lorne Whitehead that conclude that in the Domino Effect, each domino can knock over a domino 1.5x its size. To put that into perspective a domino 5mm high and 1mm thick could theoretically knock over the Empire State Building using only 29 progressively larger dominos.

If these concepts are correct, imagine how your daily habits, actions, and even thoughts can affect you in your daily life or on the course. The tiniest idea of victory or defeat passively passing through your mind can change who you are without you even knowing it. This is because your thoughts become actions. Your actions become habits, and your habits become YOU.

This is so important on the course because every time you step up to throw your disc off the first tee-box, your thinking is already determining the success of your entire round. If you step up with the idea that you will have an excellent round, your chances are much better of this coming true because your idea will manifest itself through your actions. You know you have practiced. You know you have

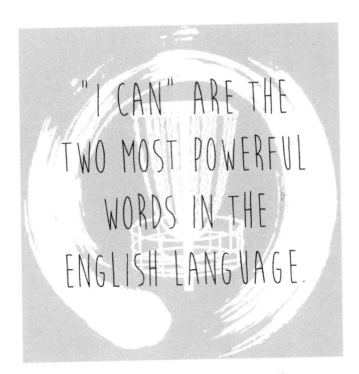

"I CAN" ARE THE TWO MOST POWERFUL WORDS IN THE ENGLISH LANGUAGE.

what it takes to throw pars, birdies, and even aces. The rest is up to your mind to allow your body to follow through.

If you step up to the tee box with a defeatist attitude, saying to yourself "I hate this hole," you will follow through in a similar trend. If you allow one poor shot to dictate the rest of your game, you have already lost. I have seen this on the course time and time again.

We all have feelings and emotions while playing disc golf, angry when we have missed a putt or discouraged when the wind blows our drives in the wrong direction. However, we must realize that how we think and feel directly affect how we throw. The objective is to become mindful of your thinking and correct it before it sends you on a slippery slope.

The first step to doing this is to watch your thoughts. Before you even walk on the course, you should be monitoring your thinking and asking yourself the critical question - "Is this thinking productive for me?" If it is not, you need to take a step back and change it.

The best way to change your thinking or to correct your unproductive thoughts is with affirmations. If you feel yourself stepping up to your shot and you notice your internal-self saying "This is a long putt. I rarely ever make them from this distance," quickly modify your thought to "I have made putts from this distance before, I can do it again." "I can" are the two most powerful words in the English language.

When you follow these steps and watch your thinking, correcting your negative thoughts with affirmations, you are reprogramming your brain. The brain works by sending electric impulses through different neuron-pathways connecting words, concepts, and emotions. Once linkages have been made your mind tells your body what actions need to take place to create outwardly what you are thinking inwardly. You can see how a defeatist attitude sends your arm a message to miss your shot. These pathways have been passively grafted into your subconscious thinking overtime, mostly without your consent. To change the way you think, the brain must disconnect old pathways like unplugging wires and reroute them into new connections. This explains why correcting lousy thinking on the spot through affirmations is so useful.

Everyday we make choices to succeed or choices to fail without even knowing it because many of us are not mindful of our thinking patterns. We may not even notice that our thinking is causing us to fail at work, home, or at play. This is why taking up some mindful practice is so essential in our daily lives.

We are our own worst critics. We are quick to program our subconscious in ways that are entirely unproductive in our lives. Everyone has challenges, problems, stresses and everyone fails at something in life. If you are on auto-pilot, you won't notice that every time something in your life isn't exactly perfect you feel like you failed and you tell yourself you are a failure. This is simply false. One of the most important things you should reprogram into yourself is "JUST BECAUSE I FAILED AT ONE THING, DOES NOT MEAN I AM A FAILURE." Disc golf is played on 18 holes, not just 1. Life is a game played 365 days a year upwards of 90 years. That is 32,850 days to improve yourself. One bad day is a drop in the bucket.

Disc golf is the perfect mindfulness practice if appropriately used. It helps you notice how your thinking, attitudes, and habits are either hurting you or helping you in your life. Moreover, if you become attuned to correcting the things that hurt you on the course, without a doubt those corrections will continue into your day to day life and just like the butterfly effect or the domino effect, they will create exponential personal growth and positive change.

LEAVE EVERYTHING
BETTER THAN YOU FOUND IT

"You can have everything you want in life, if you will just
help enough other people get what they want."
- Zig Ziglar

Our disc golf courses are the beautiful refuges where we are
able to get away from the grind of our everyday lives. It is
where we "grow taller by walking with the trees" as Karl
Wilson Baker so eloquently put it. It is of the utmost
importance as serious disc golfers that we respect our
courses as we would respect a great teacher. Our courses
themselves are some of our most excellent teachers, they can
teach us everything we want to know if we just take the time
to pay close attention. They can even be a mirror of
ourselves, but they are the also the most massive projection
to outsiders about our disc golf community.

We often talk about growing the sport, bringing in new players, wanting to see our disc athletes on TV or even at the Olympics. We get angry when people do not respect our sport, calling it "Frolf," and thinking that we are all just grown men and women playing a children's game in the woods. If we want disc golf to be respected as a sport, it must begin with us. We must, ourselves, show the sport the respect it deserves starting with the upkeep of our courses. We must project the image we want the sport to have, and we must make sure our disc golf courses always emanate the same beauty to non-disc golfers as they do to us.

What I am talking about here is that firstly we must stop damaging our courses and our sport's reputation with litter and graffiti. We must clean up our image so that our sport may grow. This must be done both pro-actively and reactively. This means: 1) We do not litter, 2) When we see other people doing these things, we make it known that it is not acceptable, and lastly 3) If we see something that should not be, we need to clean it up. Sure, we are not everyone else's maid or janitor, but we are the caretakers of our environments wherever we are.

How many times have you played a round and found aluminum cans resting on the ground near a trash can and just played on? You may have even inwardly or outwardly expressed disapproval. But did you bend over and fix the problem? Or did you use the excuse that it was not your job?

I want to make the case that it is, in fact, your job, because the disc golf course is a smaller representation of your world. The course represents just as much of your outer world as your inner world. They are two sides of the same coin.

If shown a quarter, we don't merely see either a head or a tail separately, we just see a quarter. One coin two sides, the same piece of copper-nickel alloy. Your outer world is a manifestation of your inner world. Your thinking, feelings, and emotions all manifest themselves in your surroundings and the people you choose to keep around you, whether it is your home or your disc golf course. And vice-versa your surroundings have a direct effect on your thinking, feeling, and emotions. Two sides - same coin.

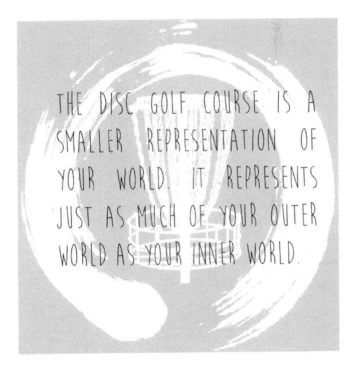

THE DISC GOLF COURSE IS A SMALLER REPRESENTATION OF YOUR WORLD. IT REPRESENTS JUST AS MUCH OF YOUR OUTER WORLD AS YOUR INNER WORLD.

Because of this, we should pay close attention to how we treat our environment because how we treat our environment is how we treat ourselves. We are an environment unto itself. We are a network of cells, organs, and organ systems all working together to become us. Likewise, the world is a network of biological cells and systems that produce life. We are not merely born into this world, we are born out of it. We are a part of it. And how we treat the world around us is an extension of how we treat ourselves. The disc golf course is just a small representation of this, but it is also our refuge and our sanctuary. It must be shown even more respect if we ever want to "grow the sport."

The next time you see those cans on the ground, don't just grumble, pick them up. You have not only done your part to clean up the course, but you have also done your part in growing the sport, and if I may get a little metaphysical, in some ceremonial way - when you cleaned up those cans you made an effort to clean up something that is going on in your internal world. Everything has a butterfly effect and doing the right thing creates both internal and external results. Maybe it made you feel like you did some small thing that made the course more enjoyable for the next group behind you. On one side of the coin, it made you feel good because you did the right thing and on the other side of the coin you saved the next group from seeing garbage all over the ground.

And this needs to manifest outwardly into our daily lives. The realization that everything around us is a representation of what is happening inside us is a powerful one because it is a vicious cycle. When we are depressed, the house gets dirty. When the house gets dirty, we get depressed. A Zen Master was once asked "How can we save the world? How can we create world peace?" The Zen Master responded, "Mop the floor." Even though sometimes we cannot see the effect we have on the universe, the little things we do add up, just as the smallest pebble dropped in the ocean creates massive waves miles away.

This is not only an environmental idea. The key here is that if each of us leaves everything better than we found it, we all can make massive improvements in the world and within ourselves.

It's not just picking up garbage. It's how we interact with people. It's how we do our jobs. It's how we raise our children. We should always strive to leave EVERYTHING better than we found it. If you attempt to leave everything better, then you will never allow anything to become worse. And many times, the little things we do are even more important than the big things that we do. Little things done daily multiply much faster than doing a single significant thing occasionally. It could be something as small as a smile and a wave to someone you don't know. It could be a compliment to someone who might be having a bad day. It could just be holding the door for someone. Some people call it karma. I call these activities "investments in the spirit" because investing means making small deposits that over time return to you in a much more substantial measure than you initially gave.

CHASING THAT
PERFECT FLIGHT

"Don't wish it were easier, wish you were better."

- Jim Rohn

I have often said to new disc golfers "Once you hear those chains, it's all over." Disc golf has a strange ability to turn any newbie into a crazed disc golf addict with only one or two rounds. But it is not only the chains that bring us back again and again. It is chasing that perfect flight. Hitting that extra long putt. And of course, the ultimate win for any disc golfer, hearing those chains ring from the tee pad.

In a way, disc golf is a lot like surfing. There is a particular spiritual "flow" to the game that brings disc golfers out to the course day after day. Just like surfers spend their lives chasing a ride on the perfect wave, we go from course to course and disc to disc chasing that perfect flight. And when it happens, when that disc is in the air taking the flight path it

97

was intended for, time seems to slow down. For some reason, we get a mild high from this. For those few seconds, time stands still, and all that matters in the world is a spinning disc in the wind. Everything in our mind is at peace, and when the disc lands, we want to do it all over again.

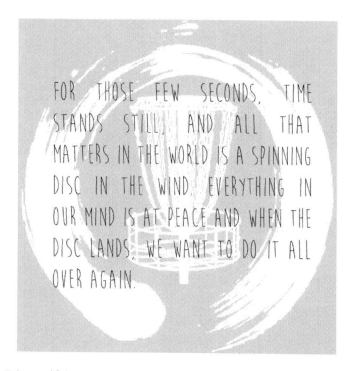

FOR THOSE FEW SECONDS, TIME STANDS STILL, AND ALL THAT MATTERS IN THE WORLD IS A SPINNING DISC IN THE WIND. EVERYTHING IN OUR MIND IS AT PEACE AND WHEN THE DISC LANDS, WE WANT TO DO IT ALL OVER AGAIN.

Disc golf brings our mind into the moment. If our mind is anywhere other than on the course, we know it hurts our game. On the course, with practice, we become able to focus on what is essential – putting this disc in that basket. How often though do we walk around from day to day like a zombie thinking about everything else but being in the moment? And what can disc golf teach us about how this not only hurts our game but hurts us in our lives. We know that half-heartedly lobbing a disc somewhat toward the basket only costs us strokes. We take time on the course to prepare our focus and our shots, carefully planning and eliminating distractions. What are we doing off of the course to develop our attention, to be in the moment, and not merely throwing ourselves passively into other vital tasks?

Chasing that perfect flight is about being in the moment and bearing witness to the fantastic things you can accomplish in life. It is finding "flow" in all that you do. It is becoming an active part in your game and in your life instead of just a spectator. This is Zen and the Art of Disc Golf.

NOW STOP READING AND GO THROW!

SPECIAL THANKS

When I began writing this book I had no idea the positive reinforcement that I would receive from the disc golf community. All of your kind words and actions have kept me going writing this. I spent many days tapping on keys instead of getting outside and throwing because I felt like what was written here needed to be poured out. Someone out there needed to read this. Maybe many needed to, but if I have improved just one person's life (or even their day for that matter) through expressing my odd little "disc golf philosophies," these three years of writing this book has been worth it. The following people went above and beyond, assisting me in getting out my message out their through social networking without even knowing who I was. For that thanking them inside this book is the least I could do!

Thank you:

@sthflagrl, @wolfmanjackflow, @messnerd, @cappaholic, @7jmblair, @mariusnaess73, @delt_nikolas, @michiganderik, @chuck_belschner, @mylyfe0fdiscgolf, @mattahtattat, @dc51021, @ilovesherrod, @radrza, @aiblair918, @uniteddiscgolfers, @smillerdg, @windy_citydisc, @jonathon_fritz, @_defendthecult, @nuclearspaceman, @afrojustice, @discgolfusa, @discporn, @minnesotaflight, @gdrew, @discgolfing_jon @disctherapy, @kenny53691, @dillaface, @goprodg, @blackfootcrockett, @cmelon78, @joe_throwz, @tziereis, @discgolf_1983, @zoidyoldpal, @ben_disclife, @jim41577, @dankstarpro, @jwade805hiker, @fenderphil23, @discholic, @a_ron907, @mistypoole, @phishdiscs, @jerrycurljuice, @mzoro1000, @thirsty_traveler, @nvsordo1, @benigz, @homerunhomejack, @darthvader710, @cmerge, @mostlee85, @lateralus12686, @hyzer_bomb, @jbacon90, @jluostarinen, @jcwillis07, @megaape10, @dan13lp, @bdusey, @kai_huff_bruh, @Zker0, @Discgolf808, @chrissinger, @JonJon_NG, @scottdudek, @realisticnoise @MindBodyDisc, @bowmanism @discgolfchris, @NoahSmith3D @BanginChains, @dietmason, and @GoHamDiscGolf

LIKE THIS BOOK?

Check out
Discs & Zen - More Writings about Disc Golf and Life by Patrick D McCormick

Please take a few minutes to review it on Amazon using the link below. Reviews make a huge difference in the success of this book. The more reviews it gets, the more people this book may be able to reach. I really appreciate your review, and may good karma find you!

http://bit.ly/zendiscgolf

MORE ZEN DISC GOLF:

Find *Zen & The Art of Disc Golf* online:
http://www.zendiscgolf.com

Facebook:
https://www.facebook.com/zendiscgolf

Twitter and Instagram:
@zendiscgolf